# Oh, Holy Allen Ginsberg:
## Oh, Holy Shit Sweet Jesus Tantric Buddha Dharma Road!

Photo: Roger Lewin/Jennifer Girard Studio.

Production: Bailiwick Repertory.

Serio-Comedy
by
Nicholas A. Patricca

The Dramatic Publishing Company

**NICK PATRICCA** is an internationally published and produced playwright, poet and essayist. Nick is an associate professor of theatre at Loyola University of Chicago, a playwright in residence at Victory Gardens Theatre, a founding member of the Chicago Alliance for Playwrights, a member of the Dramatists Guild, and a member of the Freedom to Write Committee of International PEN (San Miguel Chapter).

# OH, HOLY ALLEN GINSBERG:
## Oh, Holy Shit Sweet Jesus Tantric Buddha Dharma Road!

A Full Length Serio-Comedy in Two Acts

by

NICHOLAS A. PATRICCA

**Dramatic Publishing**
Woodstock, Illinois • London, England • Melbourne, Australia

Ideally, our religion and our sexuality ought to empower us to participate creatively and lovingly in the gift of life.

This play is committed to this ideal-hope and is dedicated to Cupid, St. Valentine, and all who struggle to learn to love.

"Thank You" to Steve Scott, David Zak, the Cast, and all the many other artists who collaborated on the making of this production; and to Sue and Chris Sergel and all the other wonderful people of Dramatic Publishing Company for their love of the theatre and of playwrights.

And "Thank You" double to all who have taught me and continue to teach me to love.

FOR: Scott McPherson, friend and colleague, "May Wings of Angels Sing You to Your Rest."

Nick Patricca
7 March 94
Chicago

3

# OH, HOLY ALLEN GINSBERG...

A Full Length Serio-Comedy in Two Acts
For Five Men and One Woman

## CHARACTERS

MICHAEL (French)  . . . . . . . late 20s, nurse and performance
artist, member of Queer Nation

JOSH (Kaplan)  . . . . . . . . Gerry's lover, late 40s, professor of
English at a Catholic University in Chicago,
Jewish, family from Highland Park, a Chicago suburb

GERRY (Gallagher)  . . . Josh's lover, mid-50s, born and bred
Chicago Irish-Catholic, diocesan priest of the
Roman Catholic Archdiocese of Chicago,
pastor of St. Sylvester's Church in New Town, Chicago,
a Gerard Manley Hopkins scholar

LEONOR (Beltrán) . . . . . . . . . . . . . . . . . . . . . . middle-aged,
Puerto Rican housekeeper for Fr. Gerry

MONSIGNOR BONONI  . . . . . . . . . born and bred Chicago
Italian-American, diocesan priest, an official
representative of the Catholic Archdiocese of Chicago

KEITH (Burton)  . . . . . . . . . . . . "burnt-out" AIDS physician,
WASP from Boston, mid-30

SETTING: A Unit Set that is capable of communicating the
various "realistic" spaces and times of the play—the Chicago
North Lake Shore apartment of Josh Kaplan, the rectory
kitchen of Fr. Gerry's parish, the medical office of Dr. Keith
Burton—as well as the art venues in which Michael performs.

TIME: Early 1990s, the last decade of our millennium.

Opening night for the world premiere of *OH, HOLY ALLEN GINSBERG...* was May 31, 1993 at Bailiwick Repertory Theatre, Chicago, Illinois, as part of the Pride Performance Series 93, with the following artists:

David Zak .......................... Executive Director
Matt Callahan ............................... Producer
Steve Scott ................................. Director
Kevin Peterson ........................ Costume Design
John Narun ............................ Lighting Design
Robert A. Knuth ....................... Scenic Design
Adrian Blundell ........................... Video Artist
Keith Marran ....................... Assistant Director
Mitchell Sellers ............... Repertory Stage Manager
Jill Seifert ................... Production Stage Manager

## CAST

Tim Curtis
Patrick Dollymore
Michael Goldberg
Justina Machado
Fred Schleicher
Marc Silvia

# OH, HOLY ALLEN GINSBERG:
Oh, Holy Shit Sweet Jesus Tantric Buddha Dharma Road!

## PROLOGUE

*(MICHAEL is dressed in a black leather motorcycle jacket, black boots, and a black jockstrap. A red bandana is tied around and over his head, communicating in code: "Ready for Action." MICHAEL addresses the audience.)*

MICHAEL. Tomorrow's Valentine's Day, OK, time to celebrate love, and romance, and friendship, and let's not forget sex, not some antiseptic plastic notion of sex, but the real thing, messy, full of contradictions, overwhelming. It's important. I mean, so OK, we don't always understand what it's all about, but that doesn't matter. We don't have to understand everything. *(Beat.)* Last week I saw Betsi give birth to her daughter. There was all this water and blood, a whole lot of body fluids, you know. Real messy stuff, but little Erika was there too. That's how it is, OK, life's messy. I mean you can try to clean everything up and pretend everything's all perfect, but that's all some game you're playing in your head. *(Beat.)* I mean, if you're really interested in people, if you really want to meet me, for example, well OK, invite me for a cup of coffee, or an herbal tea, or plain hot water, I don't give a shit, just so we do something together, that's all. Something where you have to get off your duff, get yourself in gear, make a little effort to be with me, the person you're allegedly trying to know. Sure it's scary, to reach out and touch for real, skin to skin, to get to know a real live living human being, a person other than yourself. *(Pause.)* I don't know what you're going to do for St. Val's day, but when I get home, I'm going to get all my friends together. We're going to tell the stories of all our best and worst love affairs. We're going to recite poems and raise glasses of the very best

9

bubbly to that impish bare-assed jokster who messes us all up, to that buff-naked pervert who makes us mad and foolish, and interesting, to Cupid, god of messy, creative love—May your arrows never cease to pierce our hearts.

# ACT ONE

SETTING: *The medical office of a physician specializing in AIDS. February 13, the day before the Feast of St. Valentine, Patron Saint of True Friendship. It is late afternoon.*

AT RISE: *FATHER GERRY and DOCTOR KEITH are already involved in a conversation.*

GERRY. TB?!

KEITH. Yes, TB.

GERRY. Isn't that one of the diseases the World Health Organization eradicated? I'm sure I saw a NOVA special on it.

KEITH. We need to do some tests to make sure, but I'm sure.

GERRY. When's David coming back?

KEITH. You're avoiding the issue.

GERRY. I asked you, When's David coming back?

KEITH. Father...

GERRY. Stop calling me "Father"!

KEITH. In the first stages, there's Anger and Denial.

GERRY. Don't quote Kubler-Ross to me. That's condescending.

KEITH. What may I talk to you about, *Mr.* Gallagher, the Decline of Western Civilization, the End of the Millennium, the Rise of Neo-Fascism, the Weather?

GERRY. The topic of conversation is: When is David coming back?

11

KEITH. I don't know. A month, maybe never. Don't you think David deserves a little time for himself after six years?!

GERRY. Sorry.

KEITH. No problem. I'm used to it. Attack the physician. Doctor Kubler-Ross failed to adequately explore this stage in her classic study on death and dying.

GERRY. I wasn't attacking you.

KEITH. Yes, you were. And yes you are. And yes you will.

GERRY. Why in the hell did David have to go now?

KEITH. Because he's a human being, that's why. It's taken us doctors a hundred years or so to admit it, but we are human, very human. *(Pause.)* Don't you ever get sick of it, sick of having to be understanding and sympathetic, and full of all the right answers? Don't you ever just want to say, "Bye bye, you'll all have to get along without me"?

GERRY. Everyday.

KEITH. Good. Now we're getting somewhere. *(Writes out a prescription.)* Take this to Illinois Masonic. We need to culture a specimen from your lungs so we know what specific type of TB we're dealing with. *(KEITH hands the prescription to GERRY, starts to leave.)*

GERRY. Is this your first job?

KEITH. Father, excuse me, Mr. Gallagher, I have a medical degree from Harvard, a Ph.D. in microbiology from Stanford. I'm Board Certified in three specializations. Would you like to read my resume?

GERRY. I wasn't questioning your training.

KEITH. For the last three years I was Medical Director of St. Catherine's Hospital AIDS Clinic in Boston. Last month I quit. This month I'm covering for David while he tries to regain his sanity. When David comes back, I'll wait tables at Roscoe's Cafe, if they'll have me. St. Catherine's AIDS Clinic was my last job in medicine, thank you very much.

GERRY. You're indulging yourself.

KEITH. Neither my genetic inheritance nor my expensive scientific training render me capable of indulging myself.

GERRY. What can you possibly know after three years? I've been a priest for twenty years. You just do what you can.

KEITH. 1.2499 people per week. That's how many patients died on me at St. Catherine's. I was so full of myself. I even got an M.S. in psychology. If I couldn't cure them, at least I'd help people die with dignity. I was a very big, very full-of-shit doctor.

GERRY. I'm sorry.

KEITH. I don't know how to make people better; I don't know how to help people endure pain; and I certainly don't know how to help them die.

GERRY. I'm sorry. I didn't mean...

KEITH *(interrupting GERRY)*. And stop saying "Sorry." It's driving me nuts.

GERRY. Doctor...

KEITH. And don't call me "Doctor."

GERRY. *Mr.* Burton, I ask you a personal question.

KEITH. Fire away.

GERRY. Are you a Catholic?

KEITH. Associated Congregational Reformed Presbyterian. Lapsed. I neither hate nor love God, that would be going too far, as would a strident atheism, or an assured agnosticism, one mustn't show any extreme emotion. Let's just say I have a mild verging-on-intense dislike for who or whatever is responsible for all this mess, including myself. No, I'm not a Catholic, but I've had two, well, make that three, Irish-Catholic lovers. They're hard to avoid in Boston. Look, I don't have to be a Catholic to appreciate the situation you're in. I do understand.

GERRY. No, you don't.

KEITH. OK, have it your way. I don't understand. I'll phone the hospital to tell them you're coming right over.

GERRY. I'm not ready to take these tests.

KEITH. The sooner we start treatment the better.

GERRY. For whom? You or me?

KEITH. Both of us.

GERRY. You're still operating out of the same arrogance that made you think you could fix things.

KEITH. Mr. Gallagher...

GERRY. Gerry.

KEITH. Gerry, you have TB and I need to know what kind of TB it is so we can handle it the best we can. Right now, I'm trying to take care of your body. At some other time, maybe, you can try to take care of my soul.

GERRY. The body and the soul co-exist, they co-create each other. They're inseparable. You have to treat both together at the same time.

KEITH. OK, I give up. Mr. Gallagher, why did you come here?...to talk theology?

GERRY. I came to see David.

KEITH. You know, I'm beginning to admire your stubborn, tedious single-mindedness.

GERRY. I'll take that as a compliment. *(Pause.)* I need to talk with someone.

KEITH. And David is your someone.

GERRY. Yes.

KEITH. Well, you can see how much I learned in my psych classes. Now it's my turn to say I'm sorry. You're right, I didn't understand. I apologize.

GERRY. There's no need. You're just doing your job.

KEITH. Yep, just doing my job. Can't wait till David gets back. You need to contact your sexual partners.

GERRY. I haven't had sex in three years.

KEITH. The virus can take up to ten years to present itself.

GERRY. What kind of a disease is this? It just sits inside you like a time-bomb, then one day all of sudden BOOM you're dead.

KEITH. You're not dead. You're very much alive. Please take the tests, so I can do my job.

GERRY. I need to talk to...

KEITH. Who? Who do you need to talk to?

GERRY. I need to talk to Josh.

KEITH. Who's Josh?

GERRY. Tomorrow would have been our seventh anniversary. We had this big fight...

KEITH. It's healthy to fight. The angry complainers live much longer and better than the quiet die-ers.

GERRY. We met on the Feast of St. Valentine, patron saint of true love.

KEITH. I don't know what David would say, but, for what it's worth: You don't spend seven years with someone and blow it all off in one fight, no matter how big. *(Pause.)* Is Josh HIV positive?

GERRY. He's never been tested.

KEITH. You mean he's chosen not to be tested.

GERRY. Yes. *(KEITH goes to his appointment book, looks through it.)*

KEITH. Well, as an arrogant, terminally full-of-shit, *summa cum laude* AIDS physician, I'm telling you Josh needs to be tested for TB and he needs to be tested for HIV.

GERRY. I told you I'll talk with him.

KEITH. How fortuitous! I'm free tomorrow evening. Seven p.m.'ll be fine. I'd prefer eight. You people here in the

Midwest eat supper too early, uncivilized. Thank you for the invitation. I'm assuming casual dress.

GERRY. What're you talking about?

KEITH. It's ever so thoughtful of you, taking pity on a newcomer, all alone, dangerously horny with nothing to do on his first weekend in Chicago, an act of mercy, really. Red or white?

GERRY. Mr. Burton...

KEITH. Keith.

GERRY. Keith, I have to check my appointment book. What if I have appointments?

KEITH. On your anniversary?! Cancel them. Nothing's more important than you, or Josh, or me for that matter. I'll bring three bottles of white and three of red: two bottles for each of us. Should be enough. Remember: *In vino veritas.* *(Again KEITH starts to exit.)* Leave Josh's address with the receptionist.

GERRY. By the way, you have an interesting but lousy bedside manner.

KEITH *(as he leaves).* Also by the way, it has been my experience that, although my Irish-Catholic lovers were exceedingly difficult, temperamental, anxious, guilt-ridden, and, in general hopelessly messed up, when, however, they took the plunge into the sexual abyss, they made the most passionate, wacky, far-out, awesome sex in the whole wide world. We Bostonian WASP queers have a word for it, Catholic Sex. *(Exit KEITH. Lights down on GERRY.)*

### END SCENE ONE

## SCENE TWO

SETTING: *The kitchen of the rectory of St. Sylvester's Parish. Later that same evening.*

AT RISE: *LEONOR is working in the kitchen. She is aggressively cleaning and, at the same time, keeping FATHER GERRY's supper hot and ready for him. She is in an agitated and angry mood.*

*FATHER GERRY enters through the door that accesses the kitchen from the outside.*

GERRY. *Buenas noches. (LEONOR does not return the greeting. She throws down a cleaning cloth, takes a pot off the stove, ladles out some soup for GERRY.)* Thanks, anyway, I'm not hungry. *(LEONOR gives him a look that says: "Shut up, sit down, and eat." She gives him some bread and cheese. He sits down, toys with the soup.)* So, how was your day? *(LEONOR clangs the pot in the sink, takes the pot of coffee, pours some for him.)* As great as mine, I can see. At least the weather's OK, clean, crisp air.

LEONOR. Too cold. How the animals going to live?

GERRY. What animals?

LEONOR. In Puerto Rico, I always say to myself, how the animals they live up there in Chicago? Too cold.

GERRY. Well, the squirrels burrow tunnels in the roof, the rats in the basement, and the pigeons nest in the belfry.

LEONOR *(ferociously wipes her hands with a dishcloth).* You late.

GERRY. I said I'm sorry. I've told you in the past, if I'm late, just leave the stuff on the stove and go home.

LEONOR. You missed the council meeting.

GERRY. Oh, shit. Excuse me.

LEONOR. I been working for priests a long time. I know they say worse than that.

GERRY. I went for a walk by the lake.

LEONOR. In the middle of winter! You should no do that.

GERRY. I have a lot on my mind.

LEONOR. Too cold. Not good for you.

GERRY. I needed to think.

LEONOR. Think here where it's warm.

GERRY. I can't think here. The lake helps me to think.

LEONOR. I know what's going on.

GERRY *(cautiously)*. What does that mean?

LEONOR. What're you doing with that man?

GERRY *(on the edge of alarm)*. What man?

LEONOR. He's no good.

GERRY *(a gambit in the hope of figuring out what she knows)*. You don't even know him.

LEONOR. I know him plenty.

GERRY. Leonor, I'm not following this.

LEONOR. Am I not Catholic, like you?

GERRY. Of course, you're a Catholic.

LEONOR. So why I pay rent to that man?

GERRY. Rent? Josh doesn't own any apartment buildings.

LEONOR. Why you talking about apartment buildings? For an educated man, sometimes you make no sense.

GERRY. Sorry, just trying to understand.

LEONOR. The Irish don't pay rent. The Germans don't pay rent. Even the Polish people, they don't pay no rent. Why?

GERRY. Leonor, everybody pays rent.

LEONOR. No. Not true. We all brothers and sisters, same God, we all children of the same God, we all belong to same Church. Why I pay rent? Why?

GERRY. Ok, I give up, Why?

LEONOR. *La Misa,* to have the Mass, we pay rent to that man. In the basement, and if you not finished by ten o'clock, he shut off the lights.

GERRY. Leonor, please take pity on me, I haven't the slightest clue as to what you're talking about.

LEONOR. Monsignor Baloney...

GERRY. Baloney?

LEONOR. Your friend, anyway he say he's your friend, I don't know if he is your friend, he's coming to see you.

GERRY. Baloney? Monsignor Baloney? Oh my God, Bononi!

LEONOR. All day he call. Where is he? Where is he? Where my friend Father Gerry?

GERRY. What the hell does he want to see me for?

LEONOR. That's exactly what I ask myself. And that's what I trying to tell you.

GERRY. Well, you're doing a helluva job.

LEONOR. Monsignor Baloney, he's coming...

GERRY. Bononi, Monsignor Bononi.

LEONOR. I know who he is. Why you telling me this? I know this man plenty.

GERRY. Sorry.

LEONOR. At Blessed Sacrament, he make us pay him rent for *La Misa.*

GERRY. In the basement.

LEONOR. Exactly. Then, he close the church. Not enough Catholics. I Catholic. My friends Catholic. But he close the church. Monsignor Baloney, he can't find Catholics. I go with my friends to St. Theresa's. No rent. No mass in basement. Good church. Good priests, like you.

GERRY. Thank you.

LEONOR. So what you think happen?

GERRY. No, no, don't help me. If I can do the *New York Times* crossword puzzle, I should be able to figure this out.

LEONOR. Why you talk about New York? We talking about Chicago.

GERRY. I got it. Monsignor Baloney, he came and closed your church.

LEONOR. You right. Monsignor Baloney, he come and he close the church.

GERRY. No Catholics.

LEONOR. You right. No Catholics. Only Puerto Ricans.

GERRY. Don't worry, Leonor, they're not going to close St. Sylvester's. Things are different now. They don't just close a parish without talking to the people.

LEONOR. What you think, I born last week? First he talk to you, then he talk to us. We tell him, we good Catholics, we have a good church, good Mass. Then he say, I talk to the Cardinal. Then the Cardinal write a letter. Then they make you read the letter at the Mass. The letter say, Sorry, we have to close St. Sylvester's, no money, no Catholics, only Puerto Ricans.

GERRY. I promise...

LEONOR. No. Don't promise. You cannot make promise. You not the boss—*(GERRY has another coughing spell.)* Why you no go to the doctor?

GERRY. I did go to the doctor.

LEONOR. So, what he say?

GERRY. He wants to take tests.

LEONOR. What tests?

GERRY. Tests. Just tests.

LEONOR. You sure he a good doctor?

GERRY. That's the one thing of which I am certain. *(The door bell rings.)*

LEONOR. That's him. Monsignor Baloney.

GERRY. Baloney, I mean, Bononi now!

LEONOR. I trying and trying to tell you: he say he coming over now. He say he wait for you to come back.

GERRY. I'm not ready for this. What the hell does he want, anyway?

LEONOR. I already told you what he want. *(She starts to go to the door.)*

GERRY. No, I'll get it.

LEONOR. No. This my job.

GERRY. It's not your job to open the door, but it is your job to tell me in a clear, timely manner when an official of the Archdiocese is coming to see me.

LEONOR. It my job to tell Monsignor Baloney, I Catholic. This is my church too. It is no his church the way he thinks. We all brothers and sisters. *(She softens, comes close to GERRY, takes his hand.)* Nobody knows. I never tell, never. It make no difference. You good priest. *(The door bell rings. LEONOR feels GERRY's forehead.)* This doctor, he better fix you good. *(Pause.)* Don't worry. I never tell anybody about your girlfriend, it's none of their business, but if she don't take better care of you I going to have a talk with her. *(LEONOR exits to answer the door as doorbell rings again.)*

GERRY. Girlfriend? *Oy, vey!*

### END SCENE TWO

## SCENE THREE

*(This scene is divided into three subscenes alternating between the bedroom of Josh Kaplan and the kitchen of St. Sylvester's Rectory. The time of the action is simultaneous and continuous.)*

SETTING: *The North Lake Shore apartment of Josh Kaplan.*

AT RISE: *JOSH (unseen) is in the bathroom. MICHAEL is already in the bedroom. MICHAEL starts to undress. The phone starts ringing. JOSH comes out of the bathroom wearing a bathrobe. He ignores the phone.*

JOSH *(contemplating MICHAEL)*. What a piece of work is man! *(MICHAEL undresses down to his fashionably-ripped underbriefs. The phone continues to ring. JOSH shouts to the phone machine.)* No calls after nine. It's in the syllabus. *(JOSH embraces MICHAEL, carries him to the bed. The phone machine clicks on. The recorded voice of JOSH is heard.)*

JOSH'S VOICE ON PHONE MACHINE. You have reached 555-1212. This machine records for up to 30 minutes whatever you feel compelled to say. It's been my experience, however, that brief, poetic messages, preferably unrhymed and elegantly constructed as in *haiku*, for example, are the most likely to have efficacious results on the resident listener. *(The machine beeps.)*

MICHAEL *(in bed with JOSH)*. Excuse me, is this the bed of the resident listener? *(JOSH starts to nosh on MICHAEL's body.)*

CALLER'S VOICE ON PHONE MACHINE [CVPM]. Doctor Kaplan, this is Lisa, from your English Lit class...Sorry to bother you...

MICHAEL *(responding to the sexual stimulation)*. Shouldn't we get to know each other a little?

JOSH. We did that at the bar.

CVPM. ...but I just realized there's a paper due tomorrow...

MICHAEL. Right. It must've been when Madonna was whipping Prince with Michael Jackson's underwear.

CVPM. ...and you always said we should call you when we're not going to make class...

JOSH. You wouldn't, per chance, happen to have any condoms on you?

CVPM. ...or when we can't complete an assignment on time.

MICHAEL. Sorry, I left them in my other jacket.

CVPM. I can come to class tomorrow.

JOSH. How could you, the complete queer, leave home without your condoms?

CVPM. I'm going to stay up all night trying, honest.

JOSH. So am I, Lisa, so am I.

MICHAEL. You shouldn't be so genitally fixated. *(MICHAEL takes a firm but gentle hold of JOSH's head which he brings up to his face. They kiss.)*

CVPM. You can call me anytime all night to make sure I'm really working on it.

JOSH. Lisa, I don't want to call you. I want to fuck Michael, and I fear he's one of those let's hug and talk types.

CVPM. But I don't see how it can get done properly the way you like it...

JOSH. Neither can I. *(MICHAEL gets out of bed, goes to the phone.)*

CVPM. ...you know how fussy you are, always telling us how perfection is within our grasp if we'd only dare to reach out for it.

JOSH. Oh, Lisa, you don't know how hard I'm trying.

MICHAEL *(picks up the phone at the same time he switches off the phone machine).* Hello, Lisa, this is Michael. Doctor Kaplan's got troubles of his own just now, so he can't come to the phone to talk to you. Oh, nothing important really.

JOSH. Speak for yourself.

MICHAEL. You're absolutely right: He needs to learn to relax and not push so hard.

JOSH. The young leading the young. *(While MICHAEL talks with LISA, JOSH continues his search for the condoms.)*

MICHAEL. Sure I'll tell him. Thanks for being so understanding. Good luck with your paper.

JOSH. Even if I do find them, they're probably all dried out. It's been so long.

MICHAEL. Lisa told me to tell you...

JOSH. I don't care what Lisa said. Did you turn the phone off?

MICHAEL. Yes, I did, Professor, sir. Lisa said: not to worry about her.

JOSH. I wasn't worrying about her. I'm trying to find the fuck'n condoms.

MICHAEL. ...relax, have a good night's sleep...

JOSH. I don't want to have a good night's sleep. I want to fuck.

MICHAEL. ...and everything'll all work out. Lisa's real cool. I like her.

JOSH. OK, you win. We'll talk. *(Gets into bed, settles into a comfortable position.)* Do you think Mayor Daley's gay?

MICHAEL *(getting back into bed)*. I think you're a mayor behind.

JOSH. Hey, it's my question.

MICHAEL. OK, Professor, OK. I don't think so.

JOSH. Can we fuck now?

MICHAEL. No. For one thing we don't have any condoms, for another you're not giving this thing a chance to happen its own way, OK?

JOSH *(lifts the sheets, looks at his flaccid cock)*. Too late. Nothing matters anymore. All this I-Thou stuff's shriveled my peepee.

MICHAEL *(looks under the sheets)*. I think it looks cute.

JOSH. You do? *(Coyly.)* You're not just saying that, are you?

MICHAEL. No, really. *(Looks again under the sheets.)* It really is cute. It's not shriveled; it's just being its cute gentle self.

JOSH. You mean it's not all broken?

MICHAEL. It's just waiting for the right moment. *(He starts to play very sensually with JOSH's body. Gradually he moves one of his hands under the sheets to play with JOSH's penis as he gently kisses him.)*

JOSH *(coming back into lust)*. Oh, do that again.

MICHAEL. You mean this?

JOSH. Oh, yes. Oh, yes. That. I mean that. Where did you learn to do that?

MICHAEL. Now just relax, just like Lisa said. *(Goes under the sheets to play with JOSH's cock.)*

JOSH. Oh, Lisa, Lisa, you get an A, no, you get an A+, and you can call me anytime you want. *(JOSH turns out the light by the bed, leaving the bedroom unlighted. From the darkness we hear JOSH—enjoying the sex play.)* So this is what sex is like. Oh, sweet Jesus, it's been so long. Oh, Oh, Oh, yes. Where did you learn these things? Oh, Holy

Allen Ginsberg! Oh, Holy Shit Tantric Buddha Dharma Road!

\* \* \* \* \* \* \* \* \* \* \* \*

**SPLIT SCENE SHIFT**:

SETTING: *The kitchen of St. Sylvester's rectory.*

AT RISE: *MONSIGNOR BONONI and FATHER GERRY are sitting at kitchen table. They are already heavily into their conversation.*

BONONI. I need your answer tonight, Gerry, not tomorrow, certainly not Monday.

GERRY. Why? Why can't you wait? I don't see what difference a few more days makes.

BONONI. "Time is of the Essence," that's how the agreement reads, "Time is of the Essence." Tick Tick Tick Tick. Ninety days to get this whole deal packaged and wrapped with a big red ribbon. TICK TICK TICK. And you know who has to get it all done on time. And you know who they'll blame if it isn't done on time. Me. You know who called me this morning at 6:30 a.m., the Cardinal himself, and that was right after the Chancellor, and that was right after the Vicar. They're all breathing down my neck. You know what they all want to know. Is Gerry with us or against us?

GERRY. I've always cooperated with the Archdiocese and you know it.

BONONI. That's what I tell them, "Gerry's a team player. Always has been. Always will be. He has his principles but he's a team player. He can see the whole picture not just his own little part of the puzzle."

GERRY. It should go to the Parish Council first.

BONONI. It can't go there first. First we need your support. Then you can go to the Parish Council. Otherwise, great big mess.

GERRY. You're deluding yourself if you think my parishioners are going to docilely follow my advice like dumb sheep.

BONONI. I have no illusions about this process, Gerry, none. Besides, I've met your housekeeper.

GERRY. Monday.

BONONI. Ninety days. You're already costing me three days. Eighty-seven days.

GERRY. Monday.

BONONI. Gerry, it's like dominos. Everything's lined up in a sequence. Tick Tick Tick. Bang Bang Bang. You get one thing, one little thing out of sequence. No Tick Tick Tick. No Bang Bang Bang. No deal. Great big mess.

GERRY. You could've come to me before you signed the contract.

BONONI. Memorandum of Understanding.

GERRY. Whatever.

BONONI. There wasn't time.

GERRY. There never is. When it comes to the really important things, there's never any time. But your bean counters in the Chancellery always have plenty of time to go over every penny in my Parish Budget.

BONONI. It's not just money, Gerry. It's people.

GERRY. Amen!

BONONI. We have a responsibility. Justice demands.

GERRY. Justice! Don't you dare preach to me about justice? When Ken got sick, the only thing you people at the Chancellery could think about was how to keep Ken's mouth shut. You sent that creep McNamara to tell Ken you'd cut off his health insurance if anyone found out he was dying of AIDS. That's the kind of justice you Church lawyers understand. And don't tell me it didn't happen because I was there.

BONONI. We were wrong. We made a mistake. Ken was the first, as you well know. We weren't prepared. It was a shock. We didn't know what to do. It was inexcusable what we did. Now we're trying to do better. And we need your help.

GERRY. It shouldn't have to be this way: To help one group of people, I have to injure another. It's not right.

BONONI. We have to make such decisions everyday. It's called a zero sum scenario, I learned that in business school.

GERRY. This is not a game.

BONONI. The greater good, Gerry. You must decide where lies the greater good. Your parishioners can find other parishes. The Archdiocese can't afford to turn down this offer. The property values in this neighborhood have gone right through the roof. We're talking a lot of money here, Gerry, *mucho dinero.* Money we need very badly. Money we can well use to help our brother priests like Ken.

GERRY. We should be taking care of our brother priests regardless. It shouldn't depend upon some "deal."

BONONI. You gotta sell at the right moment, Gerry. Now's the time to cash in, take our money, and build a hospice. That's the scenario. A once in a lifetime opportunity. We got to do it now.

GERRY. I can't help thinking that this whole scenario, as you call it, has been tailor-made to suit your agenda which includes, among other things, keeping priests who are dying of AIDS safely out of the sight of their parishioners. God forbid the people should see their priests struggling, suffering the things they suffer, oscillating between faith and doubt, hope and despair, all at the same time. God forbid people should see their priests dying of AIDS: this is the meaning of your hospice.

BONONI *(pause)*. Monday it is then. I'll stave off the lawyers and the Chancellor and the Cardinal himself because I have faith in you, Gerry. Don't bother, I know the way out. *(As he starts to exit.)* Gerry, this thing is bigger than we ever imagined. The insurance people are killing us. We need this money. We need this hospice. And, yes, we need a place for our priests to die. It's better this way for everyone. For everyone, Gerry, everyone. *(BONONI exits. GERRY walks around the kitchen aimlessly for a few moments, then dials JOSH's phone number on the kitchen phone. It rings and rings with no answer.)*

GERRY. Shit! *(He hangs up the phone, grabs his hat and coat, exits through the kitchen door to the outside.)*

* * * * * * * * * * * *

**SPLIT SCENE SHIFT**:

SETTING: *The bedroom of Josh's apartment.*

AT RISE: *JOSH, wearing his bathrobe, is again looking for condoms. MICHAEL, wearing the torn briefs, is culling through JOSH's poetry collection.*

MICHAEL. You sure have a lot of poetry.

JOSH. I should. That's what I teach, Einstein. Dammit, where are they?! They've got to be here somewhere. *(To MICHAEL.)* Where would you put condoms?

MICHAEL. You've got to learn to have orgasm with your whole body, not just your dick.

JOSH. I'm sure you've got a great deal to teach me. And I'm eager to learn.

MICHAEL *(discovering a collection of GMH's poetry)*. Gerard Manley Hopkins. I haven't read him since high school. Kinda strange dude.

JOSH. Just your run-of-the-mill, frustrated, queer poet, priest, neither the first nor the last of his noble lineage.

MICHAEL. One of your specialties?

JOSH. No way. Not my type. But I am very intimate with one of Father Gerard's soul brothers who simply adores him.

MICHAEL *(quoting a poem of GMH's)*. "Trees by their yield// Are known, but I—// My sap is sealed,// My root is dry.// If life within// I none can shew// (Except for Sin),// Nor fruit above—// It must be so—// I do not love." What a sad thing for a poet to say: I do not love.

JOSH *(pulls out a supply of condoms from inside one of his briefcases)*. I knew I had them! Super sensitive, super strong. A twelve pack! That should last us the night, don't you think?

MICHAEL. I thought we were going to read our favorite poems to each other, or is that what you say to all the boys to lure them into your bed?

JOSH. Hardly, I save that line for heavy duty special cases such as yourself. Rules of the House: One poem after each orgasm. Beats smoking cigarettes.

MICHAEL. You already had an orgasm, or does only fucking count?

JOSH. Normally, under House Rules, only fucking counts, but since it was such a fantastic orgasm, it counts.

MICHAEL. Good. So now we read a poem. *(Goes for his backpack which contains poetry books.)*

JOSH. You just read a poem, Einstein, remember: "My sap is sealed,// My root is dry." Poor bugger, adrift in a sea of laddies, and couldn't wet his beak. "Phalluses, phalluses, or phalli if you're classically inclined, everywhere,// And not a cock to suck.// Phalli, phalli everywhere// and nar' a lad'll fuck."

MICHAEL. Very original.

JOSH *(starts to open a condom)*. This is so exciting. I hope I remember how to do it. You can't forget, can you? It's like riding a bicycle, isn't it? Once you've learned, you can do it forever.

MICHAEL. Aren't you assuming a lot?

JOSH. Yes. I'm assuming you're a normal red-blooded hot and horny all-American boy next door queer ready for action.

MICHAEL. I am, but who said you were going to be on top.

JOSH. Ah...I'm older than you.

MICHAEL. That's age-ist. I'll report you to Lisa for public denouncement.

JOSH. I've got a hemorrhoid. Honest.

MICHAEL. Let me see it.

JOSH. It's internal.

MICHAEL. No problem. Or, have you forgotten, Einstein, that I happen to be a nurse. And assholes are my specialty.

JOSH. Excuse me, but I find it difficult to compute nurse and performance artist at one and the same time in one and the same person.

MICHAEL. The one complements and pays for the other. Bend over.

JOSH. Young man, I have a Ph.D. from the University of Chicago, I'm a fellow of Christ's College, Oxford, and I teach at Loyola University of Chicago. You're supposed to accept the authority of my word.

MICHAEL. That's authoritarianism. I'm warning you, one more *ism* and I'm for sure calling Lisa

JOSH. It's really a great indignity to make a horny old man beg, but, if I must, I must: Oh, please, fair youth, please take pity and let me be on top, just this once, pretty please. Besides it's the Sabbath and it's a *mitzva* for a Jew to fuck on the Sabbath—but only if he's on top.

MICHAEL. It's not the Sabbath until tomorrow at sunset.

JOSH. A mere technicality.

MICHAEL. I thought you mature men were more spiritually oriented. I thought you set aside the ways of the flesh for the life of contemplation. Besides, older men have trouble coming more than once.

JOSH. That's malicious sex-negative gossip. Talk about being age-ist. *(JOSH wrestles MICHAEL to the bed, starts tickling him.)*

MICHAEL. OK, OK! We'll fuck.

JOSH. Oh, thank you, sweet Jesus! This is almost enough to make me a believer.

MICHAEL. But...

JOSH. Do you spell that "but" with two t's or one.

MICHAEL. That's almost as clever as the *mitzva* ploy. But first a poem. *(Takes a volume of poetry from his backpack.)* I've brought my priceless collection of 11th-century monastic homoerotic verse, written in Latin, proto-French, and proto-Italian. I'll translate for you.

JOSH. How kind.

MICHAEL. "Whither thou goest, there my love is./ Whither I goest, there your love is./ Together like hot wax to sealing stamp/ Our hearts embrace."

JOSH. I prefer Ginsberg. He writes in good American English, and he comes right to the point, no pussyfooting like your monks.

MICHAEL *(removes his briefs, lies across the bed).* "Your letters enter my heart/ like a lover to his lover's bed./"

JOSH *(contemplating the naked MICHAEL)*. A Ginsberg poem wallows in the succulent grit of the really real: pecs, biceps, cock, balls, beauteous ass, pure poetry. *(Overcome with lust, JOSH falls upon MICHAEL.)*

MICHAEL. I'm not finished.

JOSH. Neither am I. *(JOSH reaches for the light at the side of the bed. MICHAEL relaxes, lets the volume of poetry fall to the floor. JOSH turns the light off.)*

MICHAEL. Hey, you're supposed to warm me up first.

JOSH. I did warm you up. Next to the Tantric Buddha, Ginsberg's the greatest warm-up in the known universe.

MICHAEL. Lesson #1: take your time and enjoy.

JOSH. Hold the critique until we're finished. The mere mention of Ginsberg's name sends me into warp drive. Oh, Holy Allen Ginsberg.

*(The door to the apartment opens up. GERRY enters, all bundled up against the cold. He carefully unwraps himself.)*

JOSH. Oh, sweet Jesus! I'd almost forgotten how good it is.

GERRY *(goes to the bedroom door)*. Josh. *(GERRY opens the door.)*

JOSH *(as he climaxes)*. Oh, Holy Allen Ginsberg...

GERRY. Josh, are you awake?

JOSH. Oh, Holy Shit Tantric Buddha Dharma Road. Say "YES" to Life! *(GERRY turns on the overhead lights. JOSH and MICHAEL are under the sheets.)*

GERRY. Josh, we've got to talk.

JOSH *(after a panting interval)*. In case you didn't notice, I was having an orgasm.

GERRY. I noticed.

MICHAEL *(turning his head toward GERRY)*. Father Gerry!

GERRY. Michael!

JOSH. *Oy, vey! (As JOSH gets up off MICHAEL, he covers himself with the robe.)* Please don't tell me Michael's another queer Catholic priest.

GERRY. Michael works for Doctor David.

JOSH. So what. He could still be a priest or a brother or whatever. You people are everywhere. *(MICHAEL takes the bed sheet to cover his nakedness. [From this point on, MICHAEL puts on his street clothes with the intention of leaving as fast as he politely can].)*

MICHAEL. I am a Catholic, more or less, but I'm neither a priest nor a brother nor a nun, just your regular run-of-the-mill queer Catholic lay person.

JOSH. Thank you, sweet Jesus, another Catholic cleric and this poor secular Jewish atheist would've lost his faith. *(To GERRY, as an aside, more or less.)* What the bloody fuck are you doing here?

GERRY. I need to talk with you.

JOSH. It couldn't wait till tomorrow?

GERRY. No, it couldn't.

MICHAEL. It is tomorrow. Technically speaking. One minute after midnight. *(Pointedly to JOSH.)* I don't sleep with married men. You should've told me.

JOSH. Gerry's married to God.

GERRY. Michael, I'm sorry you're getting caught in the middle of all this.

MICHAEL. No problem. I needed the practice anyway. Quick outfit changes for my performances.

GERRY. I don't want you to leave with the wrong idea.

JOSH. Oh, that's rich! Of the ever so many wrong ideas that abound here, which one in particular do you want eliminated?

GERRY *(to JOSH)*. I'm not worried about what he thinks of me. I'm trying to make things all right for you. *(Pause.)* I'm sorry I interrupted your time together. I tried phoning you but there was no answer.

JOSH. The phone's unplugged. For obvious reasons.

GERRY. Michael, Josh and I...*(MICHAEL stops dressing to listen to GERRY. JOSH moves out of the way. MICHAEL and JOSH both stare at GERRY, waiting for him to finish his sentence.)* Josh and I...

JOSH. Well, now that's all cleared up, I guess I'll take my after-sex piss.

GERRY. Josh and I...have an understanding.

JOSH. Excuse me, you have the understanding part, I have the accepting part. Correction: I used to have the accepting part.

GERRY. You certainly didn't waste any time. I hope you used a condom.

JOSH. Of course, I used a condom. Gerry, even for you, this is pretty nutso neurotic. If Michael gets pregnant, I promise we won't get an abortion. And, if he wants, I'll do the right thing by him and marry him, unlike some people I know.

GERRY. Josh, I'm not in the mood for your clever caustic asides.

JOSH. For me to throw myself at Gerry's feet and beg him to marry me used to be the high point of our anniversary festivities.

MICHAEL *(to GERRY)*. You don't need to explain anything to me. I'm sure you're here for a very good reason.

JOSH *(to GERRY)*. I know his reason: it's called "Catholic sexophobia," or, "If I can't enjoy sex, I'm going to make sure you can't either." *(To MICHAEL.)* Before I met Gerry, I thought Jewish Guilt ranked first in the hierarchy of guilt trips.

MICHAEL. It's all part of our Irish-Catholic heritage. I'm learning to have fun with it. *(GERRY notices the opened Gerard Manley Hopkins portfolio.)*

JOSH. You should write a "how to" book on sex for guilt-ridden Catholics. Guaranteed best seller.

GERRY. Sex is important to Josh.

MICHAEL. Sex is important. OK, I get it, you're the Gerard Manley Hopkins scholar Josh said he was intimate with.

JOSH. That's my Gerry. "Spring is Sprung, the Bell is Rung, the Laundry's Done." The miraculous in the everyday.

MICHAEL. Were you named after him?

GERRY. Hardly. Hopkins was English. I was named after an uncle who was a priest in Ireland.

MICHAEL. I'm glad you write poetry.

GERRY. I try to write poetry.

MICHAEL. I'd love to read your work.

JOSH. Gerry doesn't show anyone his work. I myself have been privileged to see but a few fragments of these rare objects as I clean the house or carry out the trash.

GERRY *(to JOSH)*. You've never cleaned a thing in your entire life, and I empty the trash. *(To MICHAEL.)* Josh reads my diaries without my permission.

JOSH. All's fair in love and poetry.

MICHAEL. I'd really like to read your work sometime, I mean when it feels OK. Maybe I could use your poetry in my performances.

GERRY. Thank you, but I'm afraid Josh is right. I'll never show my work.

MICHAEL. Why?

GERRY. I guess I'm afraid.

MICHAEL. Every good artist is afraid.

GERRY. Poetry is the only part of my life that's...mine.

MICHAEL. All art is intimate. That why it's important.

GERRY. Despite what Josh says, I'm not that good.

JOSH. Your poetry is more than good; it's damn good. I should know because I write bad poetry and I can tell the difference. That's why I'm a professor.

MICHAEL. I know how you feel about showing your work, but you've got to understand how much we need each other. You really don't have a choice about this. It's a gift. The whole thing's a gift. It's not about your ego or my ego, no matter how much ego we've got mixed up in it, and that's OK too, I mean, the ego has its proper thing to do, but when it all comes together, when it really works, it's beautiful. You know it's right, and the people there with you, they know it's right. It's the most beautiful and powerful and intimate thing there is. So what if it hurts, it's how we come to feel each other and know each other. It's beautiful.

JOSH. Like sex.

MICHAEL. Like sex.

GERRY. Like love.

MICHAEL. Yes, like love. *(As he exits.) Ciao!*

GERRY. *Ciao!*

JOSH *(as he waves goodbye).* It was nice while it lasted. Precocious bugger, that one. *(He starts setting things in order, so he and GERRY can go to sleep.)*

GERRY *(not forcefully enough to break through JOSH's active ignoring of GERRY).* Josh.

JOSH. Little creepy how together he is.

GERRY. Josh.

JOSH. He'll never fuck with me again. I know what he'll say. He'll say: let's be friends. God, I hate when they say that. What does that make "friendship"?—the consolation prize?

GERRY *(explosively).* Josh!

JOSH. What the hell are you doing here?

GERRY *(pacing nervously around as he speaks)*. I went to see David, but David wasn't there. This other doctor was there. That already threw me off balance. Keith, Keith Burton's his name, he's from Boston, he's helping David out until David comes back...and I don't even really know why David's away. I don't know if he's on vacation, or having a nervous breakdown...

JOSH. Gerry, just listen to yourself, especially the words "nervous breakdown."

GERRY. My god, what if David's gotten sick. Here I am all concerned about myself. Josh, they'd tell me if David were sick, wouldn't they?

JOSH. Gerry, I've been meaning to bring this up for some time now, but the right occasion never seemed to come around. I can see now I made a mistake. Gerry, it's time for you to see a shrink.

GERRY. I don't need a shrink, or even if I do need a shrink...you're not listening.

JOSH. One week ago you told me you never wanted to see me again. Then in the middle of the night, in the middle of my first fucking sexual encounter since...Holy Allen Ginsberg! I can't even remember, it's been so long.

GERRY. I'm sorry. I should've...I couldn't talk with you. If I saw you or talked to you, I wouldn't be able...I'd only cause more pain, much more pain.

JOSH *(pause)*. I've got to take a piss. I've had to take this piss since...well you know since when. *(He starts to move toward the bathroom.)*

GERRY *(takes the special portfolio edition of Gerard Manley Hopkins' work)*. You know how much I love this book.

JOSH. I know all too well how much you love Gerard Manley Hopkins. *(He again makes a move toward the bathroom. In silence GERRY starts tearing pages out of the*

*portfolio. He tears them out one at a time, very deliber-
ately.)* What're you doing? *(GERRY ignores JOSH. He
keeps tearing the pages out one at a time.)* Stop it, Ger.
You love that book! *(GERRY continues. He trembles from
the effort to stay in control of his emotions. JOSH takes the
book away from him to protect it. Pause.)* We've lost a lot
of friends. If I were religious, I'd have to light *yahrzeit*
candles everyday, every bloody day. I've had it easier than
you because I could always walk away when it got to be
too much, but you, you have to stay in it, you have to
handle a whole lot of grief and anger every fucking day.
It's too much, Ger. It's just too much.

GERRY. Doctor Burton wants to wait tables at Roscoe's
Cafe. After only three years as an AIDS physician, he's
quitting.

JOSH. Good for him. He knows his limits. When he's ready,
he'll come back. Ger, you don't know how to turn off.
Your response to more suffering is more work. There's too
much suffering out there. There's too much Sex and Death
and not enough Sex and Life. *(Pause.)* I think I've just
convinced myself to see a shrink. I'm not doing so great
myself. Now, I really must piss or I'll do it right here on
the floor, scout's honor. *(JOSH goes into the bathroom.)*

GERRY *(to himself, as he regains some composure)*. He still
doesn't understand. *(The toilet flushes. JOSH comes out of
the bathroom.)*

JOSH. OK, time for beddie-bye. Which fuzzy-wuzzy shall I
bring to bed tonight. How about Pooh Bear. *(JOSH takes
one of the toy stuffed animals, embraces it.)*

GERRY. Josh, I have TB which means my immune system is
starting to fail which means I'm going to die.

JOSH. How do you know you've got TB?

GERRY. I test positive for TB. I have to take confirmatory tests to determine what type of TB I've got and whether it's resistant to conventional treatments. Doctor Keith Burton...

JOSH. Fuck Doctor Keith Burton. Where's David? Every time you catch cold you think it's terminal.

GERRY. I don't know where David is. I wish I did. Then I'd have someone to talk to.

JOSH. You're not going to die.

GERRY. Yes, I am.

JOSH. You don't know that for sure.

GERRY. Yes, I do. Josh, I want you to get tested.

JOSH. You know full well my position about being tested.

GERRY. New treatment protocols are being discovered every day.

JOSH. Then how come you're so goddamned sure you're gonna die?

GERRY. We knew this day would come sooner or later. I've been HIV positive for a very, very long time.

JOSH. There are cures for TB.

GERRY. Josh, you need to be tested. You need to be tested for the AIDS virus and you need to be tested for TB.

JOSH. If I get symptoms of TB, I'll get tested for TB.

GERRY. I'm not as strong as you. I need to know if you're OK. I can't bear the thought that I might have...

JOSH. Don't say it.

GERRY. I need to say it.

JOSH (*places his hands over his ears*). I won't listen. I won't co-operate with your fucked-up guilt trips.

GERRY. This is not about guilt. I don't want you to get sick.

JOSH. I've got enough toes and fingers to count the times we've had sex. They were earth shattering but very infrequent events. We were always very careful.

GERRY. What if we weren't careful enough?

JOSH. Gerry, I'm really sorry you have TB. I'll do everything I can to help you lick this thing, but I will not co-operate with your hysterical notions about sex and disease.

GERRY. How dare you dismiss my concern for you as hysteria. I'm tired of taking the fall for all the problems in our relationship.

JOSH. You terminated me. I didn't terminate you.

GERRY. I thought it would be better for you.

JOSH. Do me a favor: Don't do me any special favors, thank you very much, just treat me like you would any other stray dog on the street.

GERRY. Sex is so important to you. I can't deal with it. I can't juggle my life and your life.

JOSH. That's what it means to be someone's lover. Two selves not one. Two people's interests not just yours.

GERRY. The issues I have about my sexuality express my values; they're about me, my faith, my effort to be myself. They're not sick just because they happen to differ from yours. I have to take enough shit from my Church about who I am and what I feel...

JOSH. Try lying in bed next to someone night after night after night, being afraid to touch him because he might feel you're the devil tempting him to betray his God. Yes, I think you're more than a little *mishuga* about sex, but I wouldn't have stayed with you for six years and fifty-one weeks if I didn't...if I didn't...Oh, forget it!

GERRY. Apart from David, you're the only friend I have.

JOSH. You have a unique way of expressing friendship.

GERRY. You're the only person I ever fully trusted. I don't have anyone else I can go to. Josh, I'm sorry. I was wrong to push you out of my life.

JOSH *(moves toward the bed, using Pooh Bear as a puppet surrogate for himself).* Because you're such a nice person, I'm going to let you sleep with me tonight and, before we go to sleep, I'm going to tell you one of my really good bedtime stories.

GERRY. Josh.

JOSH *(while getting into bed).* Once upon a time there was this very cute prince, and his name was Ger-Ger.

GERRY. Josh.

JOSH. OK, I'll take the tests. *(JOSH pulls the sheets over his head.)*

GERRY. You mean it?

JOSH *(from under the sheets).* Yes, anything to get you to go to sleep.

GERRY. Doctor Burton set up tests for me for Monday morning. We can take them together.

JOSH *(from under the sheets)* Why wait till Monday? We can take the tests tomorrow, I mean first thing this morning, but after I get some sleep. I don't think I can survive the weekend with you acting this way.

GERRY *(moves toward the bed).* Doesn't Pooh Bear want a good-night kiss?

JOSH. Don't you have to ask the Pope's permission? *(GERRY gently pulls the sheets off JOSH's face. Anticipating this movement, JOSH has the bear kiss GERRY as soon as the sheet comes off.)* Don't worry, Prince Ger-Ger, I won't let any bad germs hurt you.

LIGHTS DOWN—END OF ACT ONE

Interlude

*(Lights rise on MICHAEL as performance-artist Cupid, addressing the audience. He reads from a book.)*

MICHAEL. "Whither thou goest, there my love is./ Whither I goest, there your love is./ Together like hot wax to sealing stamp/ Our hearts embrace./ Without uttering a word,/ I know your love./ Without uttering a word,/ you hear my words:/ I love you."

Anselm, Benedictine monk, Archbishop of Canterbury, Saint of the Roman Catholic Church, to Lanfranc, one of his lovers.

"Your letters enter my heart/ like a lover to his lover's bed/ There they come to have knowledge of me/ To know the true love of a true friend. "

In the Eleventh Century, in an age that we characterize as dark, Anselm was an in-your-face-queer-poet-priest-bishop-saint. He wasn't afraid to celebrate real loud and in public his love for men.

Faggot: meaning a bundle of branches, as in to make a bonfire, as in to burn witches. Pansy: meaning a flower, as in fucking pansy, as if the beauty of a flower were an insult to the masculine-male ego. I mean, Where does all the hate come from? Fairie: as in fair, as in beautiful, as in good, as in creatures of the earth who know how to heal and make things grow. Queer: as in to lie at an oblique angle, as in "Sorry, I just don't fit into any of your categories." Why do I feel that the people who hate us queers really want disease and death to come from all enjoyable sexual activity? Fruit: as in delicious, as in health and life-giving nourishment, as if the ripe, luscious sweetness of life were an insult to God's creatures. And all this hate in the name of the God of Love? Anselm, where are you? We need you!

It's a wonder that any of us, queer or other, can find the way to the knowledge of the true love of a true friend.

## END OF THE INTERLUDE

# ACT TWO

SETTING: *The kitchen of St. Sylvester's rectory. It is 10:00 a.m. on the day of the Feast of St. Valentine.*

AT RISE: *LEONOR is cleaning the kitchen, keeping FATHER GERRY'S breakfast warm.*

*FATHER GERRY enters through the door that accesses the kitchen from the outside. He divests himself of his winter outerwear, hangs the coat and scarf, etc., on the clothes tree.*

GERRY. Good morning. *(LEONOR throws the cleaning cloth into the sink, takes a pot off the stove, ladles oatmeal into a bowl for him. GERRY looks through the mail that is sitting on the table waiting for him.)* Thank you, I'm not hungry. *(LEONOR bangs the bowl down on the table, pours milk onto the oatmeal.)* Leonor, you know I don't like milk on my oatmeal. *(LEONOR pours coffee for GERRY.)* Thank you but I really don't want anything right now. *(GERRY pushes the bowl of oatmeal away. LEONOR pushes it back toward him, teaspoons sugar on the top of it.)* I never eat sugar! What're you doing?

LEONOR. What her name? I going have a talk with her.

GERRY. Leonor, I don't have time for this now, and I don't want anything to eat.

LEONOR. Your woman, why she no take care of you? *(GERRY gathers the mail, starts to go to his office.)* Why you no say *La Misa?*

GERRY. Oh, my god!

LEONOR. All these years I work for you, you never forget. Never.

GERRY. I thought Father Perez was supposed to come in...I had something very important to do this morning. I'm sorry, I got things mixed up.

LEONOR. I never say nothing. Now I going say plenty. This woman, where she live?

GERRY. Leonor, it's nobody's fault but mine that I missed saying Mass today. Nobody's.

LEONOR. This woman, what's her name?

GERRY. I went to the doctor's to take tests.

LEONOR. So why you no tell me that?

GERRY. I decided at the last minute. Everything else slipped my mind.

LEONOR. What these tests say?

GERRY. The results won't be ready till tonight or tomorrow morning.

LEONOR. I still want to talk to this woman. She no take care of you right. What her name?

GERRY. Leonor, this is none of your business.

LEONOR. It my job to take care of you. It your job to take care of the people of St. Sylvester's. What her name?

GERRY. I don't have a girlfriend!

LEONOR. How many years I work for you?

GERRY. Five, six. I don't know.

LEONOR. Six years I work for you, and you never lie to me and you never miss *La Misa.* I going to find out her name.

GERRY. Josh.

LEONOR *(pronouncing the "o" as in "Joseph")*. Josh.

GERRY. Josh.

LEONOR. What kind name is this? Jocelyn?

GERRY. No, not Jocelyn, Josh. Josh Kaplan.

LEONOR. She no Puerto Rican.

GERRY. Jewish.

LEONOR. Jewish people, they like to eat plenty. Why she no cook for you? Look how thin you are!

GERRY. I've always been thin.

LEONOR. No like this. I go talk to this *(Same long "o" pronunciation, as in "Joseph.")* Josh.

GERRY. Josh as in Joshua as in Jesus as in Savior as in *(Pronounced in Spanish.)* Jesus.

LEONOR. Jesus, only men name Jesus.

GERRY. Exactly.

LEONOR. This Josh, she a man? *(GERRY nods his head.) Ay, que Dios! (Says something in Puerto Rican Spanish.)* Now I understand. *(Goes to the phone, dials.)* Don't worry, I take care this Monsignor Baloney.

GERRY. What're you doing?

LEONOR. Carmelita is *muy amable,* she very pretty too, she make good girlfriend for priest. *(Into phone.)* Carmelita, what you doing today?

GERRY. I don't want a girlfriend.

LEONOR *(into the phone).* Carmelita, *espera, por favor. (To GERRY.)* You need a girlfriend. Monsignor Baloney, he coming here. *(Into phone.)* Carmelita...*(GERRY disconnects the phone.)* This Baloney, he coming here. All morning he calling, Where Father Gerry, where my friend Father Gerry? He know something. And he no your friend.

GERRY. Monsignor Bononi wants to close St. Sylvester's.

LEONOR. I already told you this. You know why you sick? You no eat meat, you no eat milk, you no eat sugar.

*(LEONOR goes to the freezer to select a steak.)* I going make you a big steak.

GERRY. I don't want a steak.

LEONOR. And what you going say to this Baloney, I got a boy friend, his name Josh? Better to have Puerto Rican girlfriend name Carmelita.

GERRY. Monsignor Bononi doesn't know anything about Josh.

LEONOR. Then why he coming here?

GERRY. I told you he wants to close the church. It's not about me and Josh. The Archdiocese wants to sell the land and make a lot of money.

LEONOR. You very smart, but you no understand this man, Baloney. He know plenty. He want make you close St. Sylvester. He want make you do his dirty work. *(The doorbell rings. GERRY starts to move to answer the front door.)* No.

GERRY. Leonor, please.

LEONOR. No, no please. You listen to me. I take care this Baloney. I say you busy, this the day you visiting the sick. I no afraid this Monsignor Baloney. He afraid of me. I make him go away. You no ready talk to this man.

GERRY. You're right. *(Kisses LEONOR.)* Thank you. *(The doorbell rings again.)*

LEONOR. And you going eat this steak too.

GERRY. It's Friday.

LEONOR. You sick. God say, OK, Father Gerry sick. *(The doorbell rings insistently.)* Monsignor Baloney, I coming but you no be too glad to see me. *(LEONOR exits to answer the door. Lights down.)*

END SCENE ONE

## SCENE TWO

SETTING: *A classroom at Loyola U Chicago. The morning of the Feast of St. Valentine.*

AT RISE: *JOSH is giving a lecture on Gerard Manley Hopkins.*

JOSH. Trees by their yield
    Are known, but I—
    My sap is sealed,
    My root is dry.
    If life within
    I none can shew
    (Except for sin),
    Nor fruit above—
    It must be so—
    I do not love.

    Lisa, what do you think this poem is talking about? ...Well, that's certainly a clear, straightforward interpretation. According to Lisa, Hopkins is frustrated because Digby Dolben won't quote "fuck with him" end of quote. Lisa, do you think Gerard Manley would've had sex with Digby had Digby reciprocated his affection?...Definitely. You know, Lisa, I like the fact that you're so certain about things sexual, but I'm not so sure. Given Hopkins' temperament which was odd, to say the least, and the times in which he lived, the Victorian era, and considering the fact that right after penning these lines he converted to Roman Catholicism and become a Jesuit. Excuse me...that just proves your point. What then, Lisa, do you make of these lines: "If life within/ I cannot shew/ *(Except for sin),*/ Nor

fruit above/ It must be so—/ I do not love." Do you still
think one good...roll in the hay would've cured Father Gerard of his spiritual malaise?...Absolutely definitely. OK,
anybody else want to throw in their two cents? Andrew...
Hopkins hated himself. That's interesting. What makes you
say that?...Because he felt his love for men was a dead
end. Do you think that's true, that if a man loves another
man, I mean sexually as well as platonically, and a woman
loves another woman, that this type of relationship is a
dead end? Julie...It is...because they can't have any children. Is that what Hopkins is saying? Yes, Lisa...Nuns and
priests. What about nuns and priests?...Nuns and priests
don't have children. Well, at least they're not supposed to,
but I get your point, you're asking if their lives are mean-
ingful without children. Good question. Andrew...Hopkins
feels his life's a dead end because there's no way he can
show his love for men. That's pretty good, Andrew, thank
you. So, what do you think? Is Hopkins right? People who
love people of the same sex, are they necessarily trapped in
sterile, dead end relationships? Lisa...Why not?...His
poems are his children. What if you're not a poet?...Then
you're an interior decorator. Thank you, Lisa. Yes, Andrew...What do I think? *(Pause.)* Well...I think...Well,
speaking personally, I think...Today is a very special day
for me: it's the seventh anniversary of my falling in love
with a man I love very much. Thank you, Lisa. So speaking very personally, love is never a dead end. For me, the
key to Gerard Manley's poem is in the line: "I do not
love." Hopkins himself seems to have missed the real sin
and sterility of his situation. The real sin is Not-loving, to
me the Sin is everything inside you and outside you that
keeps you Not-loving. It's taken me seven years to realize
that Love isn't something you fall into or out of, it's some-

thing you learn how to do, it's an action as much as it is a feeling. When you love someone, when you get through all that other stuff we seem to need to do, like lust and power games and all sorts of stupid fantasies, when we give up our own agenda and stop trying to make the other person into what we want him or her to be, in short when you learn to love another human being, many wonderful things come to life that cannot be measured in terms of children or poems or *Better Homes and Gardens* interiors, spiritual things start to happen like friendship, and sex itself takes on whole new dimensions...when you love someone for real, and easy it ain't, I speak from all sides of that statement, when you learn to love someone, all the really important things about being human start to happen...everything comes to life just like in a Hopkins poem. So maybe Gerard Manley really did understand because his poetry attends so appreciatively to the wild, extraordinary qualities of the little, everyday things of life, the things that love alone can bring to life. On this the seventh anniversary of my love and the Feast of St. Valentine, it is my wish that each one of you finds your proper love because that's how we, as Father Gerard shows us in his poetry...love is how we become part of life itself. *(Lights down.)*

## END SCENE TWO

## SCENE THREE

SETTING: *The kitchen of the rectory of St. Sylvester's Parish—the medical offices of Doctor David. It is the afternoon of the Feast of St. Valentine.*

AT RISE: *DOCTOR KEITH is in his office. LEONOR is in the kitchen of the rectory of St. Sylvester's Parish. DOCTOR KEITH looks for but cannot find the slip of paper on which FATHER GERRY wrote JOSH's phone number. LEONOR is doing some last-minute tidying of things just before she leaves for the day. In exasperation DOCTOR KEITH phones the rectory in the hope that FATHER GERRY is there or that someone at the rectory might know JOSH's phone number. DOCTOR KEITH dials. The phone starts to ring. LEONOR is just about to leave. She answers the phone.*

LEONOR. Hello.

KEITH. Is this St. Sylvester's Parish?

LEONOR. Why, you think they close it already?

KEITH. I didn't ask if you were open or closed. I asked: is this St. Sylvester's Parish?

LEONOR. Is that what you dial?

KEITH. Yes, that's what I dialed, I think.

LEONOR. Then you answer your own question.

KEITH. Thank you ever so much. May I speak with Father Gerard Gallagher?

LEONOR. He no here. What you want?

KEITH. It's personal. He left me a phone number but I've misplaced it.

LEONOR. What phone number?

KEITH. Do you always answer the phone this way?

LEONOR. Only when I getting ready to go home. What phone number Father Gerry leave you?

KEITH. I told you it's personal.

LEONOR. You Josh?

KEITH. No, I no Josh. Who are you?

LEONOR. I, Leonor Luz Beatrize Beltrán de Sauto, Father Gerry's housekeeper. Who are you?

KEITH. Keith Joseph Burton, III. And I don't tell that to just anyone.

LEONOR *(trapping KEITH)*. You friend of Josh?

KEITH. I'm afraid I haven't had the pleasure yet, but I soon will.

LEONOR *(seizing the opportunity)*. Josh, he very nice. You going to like him. I know Josh since he and Father Gerry become friends.

KEITH. How interesting.

LEONOR. Yes, is very interesting. You know Father Gerry a long time?

KEITH. No, not really. Listen, Mrs. Beltrán, I've lost...

LEONOR. Leonor.

KEITH. Leonor, I've lost Josh's phone number. I thought I had it right here in one of my pockets. I wonder if you could give it to me. I promised Father Gerry I'd call him there.

LEONOR. *Ay, Dios*, I don't know...

KEITH. You don't know Josh's phone number?

LEONOR. Sure I know it, but I always getting all the phone numbers mixed up.

KEITH. You must have it written down somewhere.

LEONOR. Good idea. You smart man. I looking it up right here. Father Gerry, he keep all his important phone numbers right here by the phone in the kitchen. How you spell Ka-plan? *(She pronounces JOSH's last name with long a's.)*

KEITH. K-a-p-l-a-n. English is a difficult language for spelling.

LEONOR. Is not English. Is Jewish. *Perfecto!* Kaplan, Josh. 3663 Lake Shore. No too far. Thank you, Keith Burton, number 3. Thank you very much. *(LEONOR hangs up the phone.)*

KEITH. Wait a minute! The phone number!

LEONOR. I going to have a talk with this Josh. *(Exit LEONOR.)*

KEITH *(dials Directory Assistance).* Operator, would you please give me the phone number of a Mr. Josh Kaplan, 3663 N. Lake Shore? *(He writes the number down.)* Thanks. *(Begins to dial JOSH's number, then he stops.)* Fuck it! I don't want to do this. This is David's job now that he's back. *(KEITH goes to a cabinet, takes out six bottles of wine, puts them into his doctor's bag.)* I'd much rather celebrate their anniversary, and my liberation. *(Exit KEITH with wine.)*

## SCENE FOUR

SETTING: *The AIDS ward of Illinois Masonic Hospital. The afternoon of the Feast of St. Valentine.*

AT RISE: *FATHER GERRY is administering the sacrament of extreme unction to SCOTT. He is wearing a purple stole. A small metal repository of sacred oil is in his left hand. During the ritual of the anointing, SCOTT dies.*

GERRY. Scott, through this Holy Anointing, may the Lord of Life, who suffers with us, free you and all you love from all evil, physical and spiritual. May the Lord of Life, who never ceases to love us, walk with you through the mysterious veils of anxiety, and pain, and numbing confusion that darken our spirits. As Jesus the Christ has taught us: When one member of His Body suffers, we all suffer and all are in need of healing. For this reason, every true Christian strives to follow Jesus in responding with an open, caring heart to every person in need. In the manner then of Jesus the Christ and in accordance with His Spirit, by means of this sacred oil, I, Gerard Gallagher, in the name of all the members of God's Holy Body, anoint your ears with which you so carefully listen to the unspoken words of our hearts. I anoint your eyes, the light of which brightly...*(GERRY realizes at this moment that SCOTT has died. He gently shuts SCOTT's eyelids, making the sign of the cross in oil on them.)*...the light of which brightly examined our all-too human, and frequently very silly ways, always loving us, never judging, always laughing with us, showing us our vanities, both small and stupid and great and good. By means of this sacred oil, I anoint, dear Scott, your most gifted hands, the hands of a poet, whose plays show the truth about us, without cynicism and sentimentality, with gentle wit and patient love. By means of this sacred oil, I anoint your lips, the lips that kissed the lips of your lover, Daniel, who has gone on before you to prepare a place for you and is now welcoming you with an exhibit of his political cartoons protesting God's slow progress toward justice. Finally, by means of this sacred oil, I anoint your heart, the heart that would not stop loving, no matter how great the pain, no matter how great the anger, no matter how great the obstacles, the only heart that had the power and courage to open mine. Thank you, Scott, for ministering to me, for teaching this priest, this would-be helper of others, something of the art of healing, for teaching me to follow my gifts, for teaching me that it is never wrong to love. According, therefore, to the most ancient rites of the One, Holy, True God, God of all that lives, God of Life and of Death, Mother and Father of all creation, I forgive you any injury, knowingly or unknowingly, you may have caused, and likewise, in your name, I forgive anyone who has injured you. May Wings of Angels Sing you to your Rest.

### SCENE FIVE

SETTING: *The Lake Shore apartment of Josh Kaplan. Late afternoon on the Feast of St. Valentine.*

AT RISE: *JOSH and GERRY are waiting anxiously for a phone call that tells them the results of their tests. GERRY is preparing his sermon for Sunday Mass. JOSH is trying to grade some papers.*

JOSH. I'm not enjoying this.

GERRY. I'll correct your papers. You write this sermon for me.

JOSH. No, thanks. Whenever I start feeling sorry for myself being a teacher, I think of you being a priest.

GERRY. It is their decision, isn't it?

JOSH. Of course, it's their decision. It's their church.

GERRY. I understand that. I mean, am I avoiding the issue by not telling them what I think?

JOSH. Of course you are. But in this case it's the right thing to do. How do you spell "truly." After thirty papers I can't spell my own name.

GERRY. T-r-u-l-y. Some poets, however, some very good poets spell it with an "e." T-r-u-e...

JOSH *(impatiently interrupting)*. Thank you, I got it. The number of "l"s was at issue. *(Pause.)* You have the most amazing ability to address every aspect of a question except the one that concerns me.

GERRY. Sorry. You know how I am about words.

JOSH. This is definitely not fun.

GERRY. Why don't you let me read some of them for you?

JOSH. No.

GERRY. Sorry. Just thought...

JOSH *(interrupting)*. And stop saying "Sorry." It drives me nuts.

GERRY. What would you have me say?

JOSH. "Fuck you!" I'd love to hear you say, "fuck you!" Good primal Anglo-Saxon, "Fuck you, Josh" or "Monsignor Bononi, go fuck yourself" or..."Archbishop, what the fuck's wrong with you trying to take my parish from me?" ...anything but "Sorry."

GERRY *(pause)*. Josh, what the fuck's wrong with you?

JOSH. You know damn well what's wrong?

GERRY. "Josh, go fuck yourself!"

JOSH. That was entirely, totally, absolutely, definitely *not* the time to say, "Josh, go fuck yourself."

GERRY. Sor...I mean, "Fuck you." *(JOSH gets up from his desk, goes over to GERRY, takes the book out of his hands.)*

JOSH. I'm trying to pick a fight with you and you're not cooperating.

GERRY. "Fuck you, Josh."

JOSH. Ger, we're finished with the "fuck you" lesson.

GERRY. Why do you want to pick a fight with me?

JOSH. Because I'm angry, and upset, and so full of resentment that I want to punch you and/or take you out to a real fancy restaurant, the kind you never let me take you to, and seduce you with all sorts of naughty, exotic dishes and wickedly delicious deserts.

GERRY. Why does everything you want to do end up sounding like sex?

JOSH. Because you have a dirty mind.

GERRY. Why do you want to punch me?

JOSH. Because you're fucking making me sit here like a prisoner waiting for a fucking life or death verdict, that's the fuck why.

GERRY. That's a fucking good reason. I'm fucking sick of waiting myself.

JOSH. By Jove, I think he's got it. That's my fair laddie. Now, repeat after me. Let's blow this fucking joint, and go get drunk. *(JOSH starts to organize himself to go out and get drunk.)*

GERRY. Thank you for the compliment and for the invitation, but I promised Doctor Keith I'd wait here for his call.

JOSH. Doctors never call back when they say. It's against their licensing agreement with the AMA.

GERRY. Keith went to a lot of trouble to get these tests done today, because that's what we said we wanted. Whether he calls or not, I feel obligated to be here.

JOSH. Did your classmates in the seminary hate you for following all the rules?

GERRY. I didn't follow all of them.

JOSH. I don't believe you.

GERRY. Because I was such a goody-goody, I was made chief student librarian. I read all the books on the forbidden list. The censors had conveniently marked the heretical passages in blue and the sexual passages in red. Thus, my well-rounded education.

JOSH. Do I really have to go out and get blottoed all by my-self?

GERRY. I wish you'd stay.

JOSH. I don't want to spend my life waiting on doctors and test results.

GERRY. Precisely why we should wait here to know for sure.

JOSH. All day I've been thinking, what difference does it make? I was never planning on retiring to Florida anyway. I'm sure a few days here or there isn't going to determine whether we live or die.

GERRY. I need to know.

JOSH. Why?

GERRY. I don't know why. I just do.

JOSH. For once in your life, learn to let go. You're such a control freak. *(Pause.)* Sometimes, I think you fucking want to be sick because then it confirms all your guilt-rid-den, sick ideas about sex and death and punishment.

GERRY. Fuck you!

JOSH. I wish you would. *(Pause.)* Funny how we use the same word to mean such profoundly different things.

GERRY. When I was a kid, I read a story about Peter Da-mien. He was a priest who went to this island to live with lepers. One Sunday, at Mass, when it was time for him to preach, he didn't go up to the pulpit. He walked down the altar steps into the aisle, into the midst of the lepers. All he said was: We lepers. Nothing else, just "We lepers." He didn't need to preach; he didn't need to say anything more. Everyone understood.

JOSH. Gerry, what're you saying? You want us all to get AIDS?

GERRY. I'm not talking about you. I'm talking about me. I'm trying to tell you something about me.

JOSH. Sorry.

GERRY. Thank you. When I was making my rounds today in the AIDS ward, it was different. For the first time, I felt the barriers falling away. I could see through the tubes, and oxygen tents, and screens and all the distancing paraphernalia of modern medicine. I could see people. I could see myself.

JOSH. I don't want you to have fucking AIDS. I don't want anyone to have AIDS.

GERRY. Neither do I. *(Pause.)* But when the thing you most fear happens to you...it's liberating.

JOSH. Gerry, this sounds very nutso sick to me. I don't like pain, I don't like suffering, I don't like being sick, and I don't like martyr complexes.

GERRY. All my life I've lived in fear. *(Pause.)* I've never even taken you to the rectory for dinner, a simple, little thing like that.

JOSH. You needed to protect yourself.

GERRY. There's really no excuse for what I did.

JOSH. Gerry, you're a priest. You really are a priest. Some priests aren't, but you are.

GERRY. There's no shame in loving someone.

JOSH. Please. Don't do this, don't drag yourself through all this guilt.

GERRY. It's not guilt. I'm beginning to understand... Michael's right.

JOSH. You don't fucking understand a bloody thing!

GERRY. What does that mean?

JOSH. Exactly what it says. *(Pause.)* If I lose you, I have nothing.

GERRY. You have your teaching. You're a great teacher. Your students love you. They love you because you're honest with them and because you respect them. This is a wonderful thing.

JOSH. You don't believe that death is the end. I do. You've got a God and a Heaven to go to. I don't. If you die, which you seem hell bent on doing, I'm left all alone. Yes, I have my teaching. My students are great, but I don't come home to my students. I need to come home to somebody. I need a reason to come home. You don't seem to have the same need.

GERRY. I tried to end our relationship because I couldn't figure anything out, I couldn't figure out a way that would be good for you and for me.

JOSH. That's fucking why you want to die. Death is a real neat solution. No more Joshie-boy to deal with, no more Gerry-in-the-flesh to deal with, no more monsignors and archbishops to deal with, poof, no more reality.

GERRY. Just the opposite. That's what I've been trying to explain to you. I tried to cut you out of my life, but it didn't work. I thought I was doing it for you but I wasn't. I was being selfish and cowardly. Today, when I was with Scott I understood. The reality of my own death allowed me to feel, to be with him, here and now, no agendas, no unnecessary anxieties. *(Pause.)* Two weeks ago Scott asked to see my poetry. He said I couldn't deny a dying man's last request. I gave all my poetry to him, everything I've ever written. *(Pause.)* When I walked into his room, he looked me in the eye and said: you're a failure...

JOSH. You're a damn good poet.

GERRY. ...you're a failure, no matter how hard you try, you cannot hide yourself, your poetry reveals everything. And then Scott made me make him a promise. *(GERRY moves to JOSH.)* Josh, I love you.

JOSH. You never ever say those words.

GERRY. I never ever say them because they mean too much to me. Please forgive me.

JOSH. There's nothing to forgive. You are who you are. I am who I am.

GERRY. Josh.

JOSH. I'm not going anywhere. *(JOSH hangs up his jacket.)*

GERRY. I know. But you've forgotten something.

JOSH. What?

GERRY. My anniversary present.

JOSH. What anniversary?

GERRY. Our anniversary. Remember: We met, we fucked, we fought, we vowed never to see each other again.

JOSH. Seven years ago today.

GERRY. Feast of St. Valentine, patron of love and friendship.

JOSH. Ger, you know how I leave everything to the last minute.

GERRY. Not that kind of present. I don't care about things.

JOSH. You mean?

GERRY. Yes.

JOSH. You're serious?

GERRY. Yes.

JOSH. You'll say, "Yes"?

GERRY. Yes, I'll say, "Yes."

JOSH *(falling on his knees)*. Ger, will you marry me?

GERRY *(goes down on his knees)*. Yes, I'll marry you.

JOSH. Really?

GERRY. Really. I've been doing some research on it. It's called a Ritual of Friendship.

JOSH. Are you weaseling your way out of this already?

GERRY. Not at all. I intend to honor my vow of celibacy, but I also intend to honor my love for you, to make our love plain to all the world.

JOSH. Wait a minute! You mean you're going to marry me but you're not going to fuck with me.

GERRY. That's precisely what I mean.

JOSH. It's illegal. Talmudic law, canon law, and civil law are all on my side. Once you say: "I do," I have conjugal rights.

GERRY. Sue me.

JOSH. Gerry, let's get a few things straight: You took the vow of celibacy, not me.

GERRY. I'm not asking you to take a vow of celibacy. I want you in my life. I want to...I want to come home to you. I want you to be with me when I find it too difficult to be with myself. And in return I promise to make a home for you in my life. I'm asking you to publicly and solemnly declare according to a most ancient and sacred ritual that you will be my true friend and love me forever, for all eternity. *(GERRY kisses JOSH, tentatively at first, then passionately.)*

JOSH. OK, but I'm not going to repress my good old, all-American boy unnatural lust for your body.

GERRY. I'll deal with it. *(They continue to kiss passionately. The doorbell rings.)*

JOSH. Fuck 'em. *(The doorbell rings.)*

GERRY. I think we should answer the door.

JOSH *(still kissing GERRY)*. I said, Fuck 'em.

GERRY *(breaking from the embrace)*. Josh, you know how much I hate bells.

JOSH. So answer the bloody door.

*(GERRY opens the door. Enter KEITH and LEONOR.)*

KEITH and LEONOR. Happy Anniversary.

LEONOR *(kisses GERRY)*. *Felicidades!* Why you no tell me it's you anniversary?

KEITH. Leonor and I ran into each other in the stairwell. It's a long story, suffice it to say it was love from the first phone call.

LEONOR *(moves right in on JOSH, kisses him)*. Congratulations! You Josh, no?

JOSH. I Josh, yes.

LEONOR. Why you no cook for Father Gerry? Look how thin he is!

JOSH. I don't cook for myself. You must be Leonor. *(Shakes her hand)*. *Encantado.*

LEONOR. *Igualmente.*

KEITH. Congratulations, Josh. *(Holds up the doctor's bag.)* Three bottles red, three white. I'll get more for tomorrow night.

LEONOR *(to GERRY)*. Why you no bring Josh to St. Sylvester, he cute.

JOSH *(to LEONOR)*. Thank you just the same, but I'm allergic to Christian churches, I break out all over.

LEONOR. We all God's children.

JOSH. Speaking of God, *(To KEITH.)* what was the verdict?

KEITH. I didn't come here to deliver test results. I came here to celebrate your anniversary. Besides, David's back, and as of five p.m. this very day I'm an emancipated physician. Goodbye medicine, hello Roscoe's Cafe. Red or white?

JOSH. Wait a bloody minute here! I've been in an emotional wringer all fucking day waiting for your bloody phone call...

GERRY. Josh.

KEITH. I've made an appointment for both of you to see David tomorrow morning at 9:30 in his office.

JOSH. You're the one who wanted to know.

GERRY. I've changed my mind. Bride's prerogative. Tomorrow's soon enough.

JOSH. You're right. Plenty of time tomorrow for test results. Now, we're getting married!

KEITH and LEONOR. Married?

GERRY. Ritual of Friendship, developed by 11th-Century monks to celebrate homoerotic love.

KEITH. So that's what monks do when they're not brewing Benedictine.

LEONOR *(to KEITH)*. What is this "benedictine" they making?

KEITH. Fancy whiskey.

JOSH *(to KEITH)*. One red, one white.

KEITH. Yes, sir, Professor. One red, one white, coming right up.

JOSH. Now if only I can find those bloody rings we bought when we were young, foolish lovers.

GERRY. Hope they still fit. *(JOSH exits in search of the wedding rings.)*

LEONOR *(to GERRY)*. Priests no can get married.

GERRY. Neither Church law nor Civil law says Josh and I cannot declare our love for each other.

LEONOR. Nobody can make a law against love.

GERRY. *Exactamente. (GERRY kisses LEONOR. Doorbell rings.)*

LEONOR *(to GERRY)*. I answer the door. You get ready for your wedding.

KEITH. That'll be Michael. He's bringing some guy he met two-stepping at Charlie's.

*(LEONOR answers the door. Enter MICHAEL and MONSIGNOR BONONI.)*

LEONOR *(surprised)*. Monsignor Baloney.

GERRY. Baloney! Oh, my god.

BONONI *(equally surprised)*. Leonor, what're you doing here?

LEONOR *(quickly recovering from her surprise)*. I asking myself same question about you?

GERRY. Monsignor Bononi, what a surprise?! Thank you for coming. *(Kisses MICHAEL)* And thank you, Michael, for bringing him.

MICHAEL. So you guys know each other?

GERRY. Well, let's just say that because of you we know each other a lot better now, a whole lot better. *(LEONOR, sizing up the situation, seizes the advantage.)*

LEONOR *(to BONONI)*. Why you no introduce me to your boyfriend?

MICHAEL *(to LEONOR)*. Hi, my name's Michael. *(To GERRY.)* Where's Josh?

LEONOR. Josh is getting ready for the wedding.

BONONI. What wedding?

MICHAEL *(to BONONI)*. Isn't it wonderful! After seven years, Gerry's going to make an honest woman of Josh.

LEONOR *(taking BONONI's arm)*. It's OK. It's not like you think. Father Gerry, he got it from some old monks who make a very good whiskey. *(Sotto voce to GERRY.)* Don't worry. Is perfect. Now the shoe is on his feet too.

GERRY. Monsignor Bononi, this is Doctor Keith Burton.

KEITH. Nix the doc talk. Just call me Keith.

BONONI. Pleasure to meet you. *(To GERRY.)* What the hell's going on?

*(JOSH enters with rings.)*

JOSH. Found them in the heavy porn drawer under the old Drummer mags. *(GERRY goes to JOSH, takes his arm, introduces him to BONONI.)*

GERRY. Monsignor Bononi, I have the honor and pleasure of introducing to you my lover, Josh Kaplan.

JOSH. Gerry, I never agreed to a Catholic wedding.

BONONI. Nor did I agree to officiate.

JOSH. Good, because I want Doctor Keith to perform the ceremony.

KEITH *(as he prepares to hand both glasses of wine to JOSH).* I'm afraid I can't do that. God and I don't get along. In fact, we're no longer on speaking terms.

JOSH. Perfect. *(To GERRY.)* Isn't Bononi the guy that's trying to take your church from you?

GERRY. That's him. In the flesh.

JOSH. Should make things interesting.

KEITH *(offers the wine to JOSH).* One red, one white.

JOSH. As our official minister, it is your sacred duty to give us the glasses of wine after we have professed our vows.

LEONOR *(taking her place in the scene).* I no dressed right for wedding. *(She takes BONONI's arm in hers on the right, MICHAEL takes BONONI's other arm in his on the left.)*

MICHAEL. You look just great. *(GERRY hands JOSH a sheet of paper.)*

GERRY. I'll say the ritual in Latin. You repeat it in English.

JOSH. Deal.

GERRY. *Pectus amor nostrum penetravit flamma.*

JOSH. The fierce flame of love has pierced our breast.

GERRY. *Atque calore novo semper inardet amor.*

JOSH. Our love always fresh burns true and pure.

GERRY. *Nec mare, nec tellus, montes nec silva vel alpes/ Huic obstare queunt aut inhibere viam.*

JOSH. Neither sea nor land, neither mountains nor woods nor hills/ can block our love's way.

GERRY. With this ring, I promise to be with you, Josh Kaplan, in sickness and in health, in good times and bad, till death do us part.

JOSH. With this ring, I promise to be with you, Gerard Gallagher, in sickness and in health, in good times and bad, till death do us part. The rings fit! *(GERRY and JOSH kiss. KEITH hands them the glasses of wine. They entwine their hands, drink the wine. Everyone applauds, offers their congratulations.)*

KEITH *(as he offers glasses of wine to everyone)*. Toast. A toast to the newlyweds. Michael?

MICHAEL. I'm too shy.

JOSH. You mean you can't give a speech with your clothes on.

LEONOR. I think Monsignor Bononi would like to make a little speech. A special blessing.

BONONI. Ahem...well, the ways of God are mysterious indeed. He who is without sin let him cast the first stone. What you do unto the least you do also unto me. What God has joined together let no man try to take apart...or something like that. People who need people are the luckiest people. Sorry, I'm a little nervous. You should've given me some advance notice.

GERRY. None of us got any advance notice. That's how life is.

MICHAEL. Besides, if you had been given any indication, you wouldn't be here.

BONONI *(clears his throat again)*. There's a lot we don't understand. We think we're in control but we're really not. Nothing is very certain in this life. But there's one thing

we know can never be wrong: it can never be wrong to
love, that's got to be something we can hold onto...

KEITH. I'll say Amen to that.

BONONI. So, in conclusion: Gerry, Josh, love each other
well, and may I have another glass of wine.

KEITH. Of course, you earned it.

MICHAEL. That was sweet. Isn't he just a big teddy bear.
*(GERRY takes out a piece of paper, motions everyone to be
quiet and listen.)* A poem!?

GERRY *(to MICHAEL)*. It's my gift to Josh for our anniver-
sary-wedding, and it's my gift to you for bringing us together.

JOSH. Ladies and gentlemen, distinguished guests. I have the
great honor to present to you Father Gerard Gallagher making his virginal debut as an out-of-the-closet queer poet-
priest. Father Gallagher. *(Applause and shouts of welcome
from the assembled.)*

MICHAEL *(to GERRY)*. Break a leg.

GERRY.    *Young Michael*
          The animal soul
          burns
          in young Michael
          like Blake's bright
          Tyger
          scorching the night
          rousing clues
          (emergent memories
          of fatal intelligence)
          strewn
          by nature's accidental
          hand
          through thickets of fleshy mind.

LEONOR. That's beautiful. I love tigers.

MICHAEL *(to GERRY)*. Thank you.

BONONI. That was good, Gerry. Didn't think you had it in you.

LEONOR *(takes hold of BONONI)*. Monsignor Baloney, I have some church business to discuss with you, you know what we talked about this morning. I think now we can talk some real turkey.

BONONI. Gerry!

GERRY. You're on your own. I've never been able to control her.

LEONOR. This is no his business. I president of the Parish Council.

BONONI. Oh, you are, are you. You should've told me that this morning.

LEONOR. No, is better this way. Now I know you like boys.

BONONI. Please, don't say "boys," gives people the wrong impression.

LEONOR. What you call him then?

BONONI. Young men. Much better word. "Boys" makes us lawyers nervous.

LEONOR. OK, no problem, so now I know you like "young men," so now, we can go make a deal that's good for everybody. *(She grabs a bottle of wine and heads off to the bedroom with BONONI. MICHAEL steps out of the play, addresses the audience.*

MICHAEL. "The fierce flame of love has pierced our breast/
　　　Our love always fresh burns true and pure/
　　　Neither sea nor earth,
　　　Neither mountains nor woods nor hills/
　　　Can obstruct our love's way./
　　　Even time which corrodes the joy of all things/
　　　Cannot taint the heart made whole by love."

Alcuin, Catholic priest, court advisor to Charlemagne, to his friend, a bishop and former student. Alcuin, Benedictine monk, creator of the idea of universal public education, founder of the first public school system, queer-poet-priest. Ritual of Friendship the monks called it: A way to make public and sacred the love that cannot be obstructed.

*(BONONI and LEONOR re-enter the scene. JOSH goes to put on some dancing music.)*

LEONOR *(to GERRY)*. I going to get the parish to support his plan for the hospice. It's a good idea. And, he going to make sure Puerto Rican people be on the Archbishop's Council. Good deal, no!?

GERRY. Henry Kissinger couldn't have done better himself. *(JOSH grabs GERRY.)* What're you doing?

JOSH. It's traditional for the bride and groom to dance together.

GERRY. I don't dance.

JOSH. Yes, you do. You just think you can't. *(He starts to lead GERRY in a dance.)*

GERRY. This feels very awkward.

JOSH. Get used to it, because from now on we're going out dancing twice a week. *(LEONOR and BONONI start to dance together.)*

BONONI. It's really easy, Gerry. I was just like you. Michael taught me in one night. It's all in the hips. *(As JOSH and GERRY dance, GERRY starts to relax and take the lead. MICHAEL takes a glass of wine from KEITH, steps out of the scene, addresses the audience.)*

MICHAEL. To Cupid and St. Valentine, to Love and Friendship. May your arrows never cease to pierce our hearts!

THE PLAY ENDS AS THE PARTY CONTINUES

# DIRECTOR'S NOTES